AF669464

Urban Heartbeats

Monica Manolachi
and
Neil Leadbeater

Copyright© 2025 Monica Manolachi and Neil Leadbeater
ISBN: 978-93-6354-244-0

First Edition: 2025
Rs. 200/-

Cyberwit.net
HIG 45 Kaushambi Kunj, Kalindipuram
Allahabad - 211011 (U.P.) India
http://www.cyberwit.net
E-mail: info@cyberwit.net

No part of this book may be reproduced or transmitted in any form or by any means, electronic, mechanical, photocopying, or otherwise, without the express written consent of Monica Manolachi and Neil Leadbeater.

Printed at Repro.

Acknowledgements

Monica Manolachi is thankful to the editors of literary magazines and anthologies who first welcomed some of these poems into print or online: *Artemis Poetry (UK), CivicLeicester (UK), EgoPhobia (Romania), Eikon (Romania), Revista de Povestiri (Romania), The Poet Magazine (UK), Tracus Arte (Romania).*

Neil Leadbeater is grateful to the following editors of magazines and anthologies in which some of these poems have appeared: *Allegro Poetry (UK), Ann Arbor Review (USA), Areopagus Magazine (UK), CHALLENGER International (Canada), Drawn to the Light (Eire), Dreich (UK), Harvests of New Millenium (India), Letralia (Venezuela), Live Encounters (Indonesia), Long Island Sounds Anthology (USA), Optimum Poetry (UK), Places of Poetry Project (UK), Places of Poetry Anthology (UK), Poetry Cornwall (UK), Poetry Scotland (UK), Purple Patch (UK), Quarry (UK), RALM (France), Red y Acción (Colombia), Sabdha Sanyojan (Nepal), Southend Poetry (UK), Stirling Council website: Poem of the Month August 2017 (UK), The Blackcountryman (UK), The Poet (UK), The Poetry Kit (UK), Todo Literatura (Spain), What Have You Lost / Found Anthology (USA) and the Wolverhampton Literature Festival 2020 Poetry Anthology.*

Contents

I: Monica Manolachi

Bucharest

Winter Day

It was a winter holiday and we were playing Scrabble.
Calea Văcăreşti filled with a strange humming noise:
not of trams, trolley busses, car sirens,
not the clatter of hooves and carts.
It was voices chanting *Freedom, Freedom*,
the same voices as inside factories,
a long, painful, woeful echo
and I did not yet have all the letters
to lay my word on the board.

I rushed to the window and saw it all:
holding flags, their arms raised,
they strode, wearing heavy coats,
ushankas made of sheepskin, just like my grandad's.
They were heading for the city centre, but there was no
centre, not since the earthquake in '77, collapsing
all the blocks of flats, everyone turfed out
of their dreams, driven to madness or suicide,
some were just leaving with no idea of destination—
it looked like a procession, like some sort of wedding,
but with no bride and no groom.

Mother tried to phone at lunch time and tell us
"Don't go out!", but all the lines were down.
The field across the road was all snow and scars,
there was no door that could be got out of,
no more bitter cherries from sellers at the gates.
It was winter. We had to understand that.
Death. Birth. Life. All of it at once.
Heroism, we'd been taught about it for years in school
and now, here it was, happening, live, on our streets,
where we'd licked candy floss in summer
and played "What's the time, Mr Wolf?!"

The city bustled, people came and went,
as the meaning of it all sank in,
and subway trips went on forever
starting under one regime and ending in another.
In broad daylight, turtle doves fell from the sky,
black-and-white televisions blinked euphorically,
screens came alive with unexpected colours,
branches flew from the trees,
fires alive with promise lit the night.

I had left myself behind for years on end,
I would follow myself as we do now on Google,
I would say to that girl: “Hi, how are you?”
By the time the answer came, she had already gone,
separations never hurt,
I would glide across the abyss between us,
I have invented linguistic seasons,
I have and have, you have and have
dreamt, failed, resumed.

Had I been able to go out then,
I would have seen the queues snaking around absence,
I would have heard the keys turning in the keyhole,
Dacian words, *barză, varză, viezure, mânz*,
I would have sensed carbide lamps from barricades,
I would have intuited locks, dampness, rust,
the eyes of empty rooms,
the candles and smoke of a memorable Christmas,
I would have enveloped this world in evening,
I would have seen you at your window,
a polyhedron with a heart
playing non-stop Scrabble.

Le Gavroche de Bucarest

Hyphens of gunfire split the air—
parentheses of bodies curled behind barricades.
A comma of hesitation before the next shot,
an exclamation mark of shrapnel
tearing through the silence near Colţea.

I am fourteen—a verb caught between the lines,
an unfinished sentence running down Edgar Quinet.
Footsteps scatter like misplaced modifiers,
while gunfire punctuates University Square—
full stops, red and final.

Where is the predicate of this revolution?
The breadlines stretch into ellipses of waiting,
rationed oil pooling in the cold brackets of hunger.
The syntax of scarcity:

- noun—*cartofi;*
- verb—*a primi;*
- subject—*nimeni.*

A semicolon divides the ones who run
from the ones who fall.

A boy I knew from school—his body, a fragment,
his name, a censored clause in tomorrow's textbooks.
The grammar of history is rewritten in real time,
words erased before they can be spoken,
sentences broken before they can be read.

I search for a future tense
but find only shifting syllables and an asterisk,
leading nowhere, colliding with the night
of the mind.

Woman in a Blue Dress

During the June 1990 Mineriad, press correspondent
Andrei Iliescu took a photo of Izabela Odor
in the centre of Bucharest. This poem is for her.

When I wished for a real revolution,
I laid my voice on the line.
When words became meaningless,
scattering to the four corners of the world,
I wanted to be a sign in the blinded crowd.
They had gathered with clubs around me
and I shouted at them fearlessly:
What are you all doing?

I made the step, decisive and honest,
I held the bag to my chest,
as if it were the world itself,
the baby I wished to have,
my summer bag, my raffia handbag,
my summer bag like a shield
against fury and fright.

My body, a motif for heroic acts,
the greatest achievement of my life,
the photo of an unspoken truth,
animated, magnetic, resistant,
stood in the street, fearless,
and I watched them fight
for its cerulean blue beauty
like lads playing a football match.

I crossed the street when no one dared,
when they chanted on and on: Hooligan! Loafer!

Knocked down as I was, I tripped death up.
Lying on the ground, I lectured them, nothing hurt.
Underneath my summer blue dress
I also wore their blue dress for a while,
bruises on my back, my hips, my arms.
The proof of cowardice had to be preserved
in an exemplary body, hit again and again,
silenced and forgotten for 25 years.

After 25 years, children wanted to know
who the woman in the blue dress was,
who confronted brutality all alone,
who struggled for them barehanded,
who kept quiet when they were born free,
how the tangled skein of violence unravelled
and how it rolled across the borders.

A photographer got lost in the maternity of history
among the probes, pliers, dilators and scoops.
After a long transition interval,
hysterosonography proved to be useful.
For the foreign press. On the company gazette.
I gave birth to democracy, this living gift,
I gave birth to her as mothers do,
with pain and tears, with patience and love.

I have been a metrologist for years,
I have cared for measure as much as you did,
Eminescu, Arghezi, Stănescu, Brumaru,
I have kept time and sung in the square,
I have often weighed up
my wish for poetic freedom in one scale
and the unjustified beating in the other.
Today I step with dignity among sacred monsters,
baby in my arms and bag on my shoulder.

Freedom Alley

Wandering together on a long quiet alley,
one hundred new benches here and there,
we stroll from one to another, sounding out
the same word, *freedom*, carved on the wooden back
of each bench, each time in a different language.
Like a snake, the kilometre of strange signs
winds its way between rare prison flowers,
cigarette butts and children on scooters.

Lighting poles with solar panels
salute us and check the time.
Behind us, the strangers.
They murmur names of exotic flowers.
We stop; they pause as well.
We speed up, they too hurry.
We turn to them. Nobody.
Only pigweed and bindweed.

Night is falling, the dead gather in the park.
They come from all directions,
silent, familiar, ethereal,
leaving their backpacks full of stars in the grass.
They draw near the water and drink.
Some chat over shared memories.
Others make gestures from far away
like bright kites still in the sky.
Some will see us home,
open windows, doors, drawers, laptop,
and read the messages they sent to us,
recalling how much they loved us.

Truth is a bridge between our world
and the next world, a bench where

no word is written, on which you cannot sit.
Lighting poles intone foreign words
in languages we have never heard of.
We walk past pigweed and bindweed,
we listen to the incantation of the unseen,
wake up at night when we dream of them
and they, bewildered, clamour:
Who are you? Who are you?

History Test in a School from the Outskirts

My classmates closed the books and began writing.
You could have heard a pin drop.
The question was about some ancient kings.
Puzzled, I asked my neighbour for a clue.

Tommy was slim, brown-eyed,
the son of a film-maker and a typist.
They believed in the Second Coming.
He knew how history was made.

Mr. Traian came quickly to our desk.
Without a word, he slapped me on my head
and hauled me out. I was almost eleven.
Boudicca, Nefertiti, Zenobia, help!

He shut the door. I was in limbo.
I was at school, but not really at school.
I had learned the lesson, but could not prove it.
There were no kings on the corridor. Only the cleaner.

Surprisingly, the heating had come on.
Its warmth, the snow falling outside,
the cleaner's song, all these comforted me.
I turned to the door and watched its handle.

The power of staring, that must have been.
Heavy steps, a short squeak, his bony fingers.
He seemed another man, he took my hand
and, blinking, sent me to my seat.

The Rorschach Test

When the Berlin Wall came down,
the wind in Berceni was sweeping autumn leaves.
I was in year 8, had classes in the morning
and wore a blue uniform with a number on my shoulder.
I woke up early, took trolleybus 76 to Piața Reșița,
and read a few pages of Silvia Kerim on the way.
We had maths, Romanian, Russian, art and geography.
Germany was a coloured map in an atlas,
the names of clothes and toys in the Neckermann,
the children's storybook Dad read aloud to us,
Die Puppenmutti kocht or *Die drei Wünsche*,
the language in which he'd ask, opening the door:

Was machen Sie, meine Mädchen?

Twenty-five years later, I started crying first thing
in front of the class, on an empty stomach, when a student
offered her view of an old newspaper photo
lost in an English language textbook:
the stone thrown at the wall looked like a volleyball.
Let's say the poor ink from the copier was to blame—
Multiplied all ways, history becomes a Rorschach plate.
I leaned my back against the whiteboard
and found it hard to explain in a few sentences
that what seems a wrong answer wasn't really wrong,
why the past took the shape of tears
and strange wings grew suddenly on my back.

Windows

In the beginning, there were the houses.
People lived in them less than they do today.
Inside the houses, it was almost always dark.
Sometimes, a large butterfly would land on the wall
with filigree wings and many colours.
When the butterfly took flight,
its shadow grew larger and larger on the wall,
a simple calling could be heard,
and a crack would form.

That's how we, the windows, appeared.
We pull you out of the world, we frame you in it,
with curtains, without curtains.
Like the depths of water or the height of the sky,
we reflect and conceal between sand and chalk,
demolition and construction.
Both witness and accomplice,
we gently separate, with transparent love,
the little fish in the bowl from the sparrows' nest.

Like a memory from paradise,
on certain nights we dream we are butterflies
and we too take flight.
Behind us remain only hypotheses.
Ruin, forgetting, blindness, the new world's song.
The joy of closing your eyes, of seeing.
The cold and the wind one might feel.
Then the photographers come and confess:
yes, we have stolen the windows!

Whispers after Dusk in King Carol I Park

What if someone
could walk through paradise in a dream
receive a flower as proof
their soul has been there,
and wake up holding it?
What if?

Recent History

Boxes of blueberries, blackberries and raspberries.
Old boulevards gone, the Old Town born.
Bon Jovi, Depeche Mode, Rolling Stones concerts.
The founding of the independent theatre Giuvlipen.
Mint lemonade at Grădina Verona.
You and I at the same time in University Square.
The Uranus area gone, the Văcărești Park born.
A Balkan city with many hearts beating as one.
Mozart and Beethoven outdoors at Mogoșoaia.
Japanese quinces and camellias of many kinds.
Breakfast at Paul's patisserie, lunch in Herăstrău Park.
A Colombian, a Nigerian and a Nepalese
on the tram that takes us to the clinic.
Johnny Depp at Otopeni, en route to Clejani.
An ice rink in the middle of summer, bicycles jostling.
Thoughts instantly transmitted to thousands of eyes.
Who would have imagined it 30 years ago?

After the Vote

I took a short walk in the park.
A child was speaking French
with his parents.
He was on his father's shoulders
stretching toward some mirabelle plums.
Attendez!—meaning "don't move"
so he could pick the fruit.
This is Romania today.
Meanwhile, I'm grading papers:
inversions & compound adjectives
& imaginary letters to writers.
Sunday work. Side by side
with the gardeners and the street cleaners.
There's a hedgehog in the tall grass.
In front of me, a little frog
pulsing on the pavement in the sun.
It's May 2025. Life goes on.

Tecuci

Family Story

Only the beginning matters. Once upon a time, there was a young family, somewhere in the countryside, in a water meadow between two large rivers. They had a white house, and there were bushes of lilies and chrysanthemums in the garden. In the evening, the crickets could be heard. America was far away, crinolines even farther. In one room, they had a chest filled with peasant garments and fabrics. In the kitchen, water boiled in a small pot. They were making polenta. A little girl was looking at the plate with sorrel sauce. She was a little girl like any other. On that day, the war arrived. By train. In their village. Her father enlisted. On another day, the Spanish flu came. From another continent. Her mother's name was listed. On another day, the famine came. Crimes could no longer be stopped. Criteria no longer made sense. No passing here. Sacrifice after sacrifice. Coffin after coffin. The little girl was left alone. Speechless. No schooling. She was left behind. Later on, she became pregnant. Life taught her lessons. She always signed with her finger the letters that others wrote for her. I knew she had been raised by her grandparents. That tearful little girl is not me. I am the daughter of a little girl who once lived inside another little girl, herself born of that little girl who could not write. She wept, she marked the wood, she could play the fiddle on Sundays at the dance. She loved listening to music. I visited her one summer vacation. We talked like one little girl talks to another. I slept and dreamed on the bed above her oven. She gave me a plate with sorrel sauce. The crickets stitched the darkness with their cree-cree-cree, cree-cree-cree...

The Small Market from Tecuci

Melancholy is the sleep of the soul;
in the same way, sleep is the melancholy of the body.
Calistrat Hogaş

We would wake up with eyes like tiny spiders,
weaving through the vast darkness.
Grandpa loaded the bin of cucumbers
and the bucket of tomatoes onto his bicycle
and pedalled toward the motor bus,
where he placed them in the open luggage hold.

In the valley of Bârlad, the sun had not yet risen.
There were no streetlights—
not even at the main crossroads of the village—
so the passengers, waiting in the dimness,
looked like shadows, laughing quietly before dawn.

I kept my eyes on the horizon, waiting
for the first light. The new day unfurled slowly,
like a peony blooming in May,
opening with every stop the bus made
from our village to the town.

When we arrived and the bus
parked at the station, I jumped to the ground:
people were everywhere,
coming from every corner of the county.
Watch the bin, Grandma said,
handing me the bucket of tomatoes.

Only then did the young market guard
in her flowery dress stir awake.
While her grandmother crossed the street, she

stood still for minutes, like an ancient milepost
on a forgotten plantation.
The journey unstitched who I was,
weaving me into someone new.
She sent me to read the list of prices
posted on the public board.
Only after Grandma had sold a few kilos
of tomatoes and cucumbers was I allowed to buy
a conical wafer from the ice cream stand.

Within an hour, Grandpa arrived, driving
his wagon full of melons. He parked on one side
of the market and shouted
Early fruit! Early fruit! even though summer
was ending, and people were already full.

In the afternoon, I curled up
inside the now-empty bin and began
reading a shortened version of *Tom Sawyer.*
I drifted off to sleep and dreamt
that I was selling
impossible oranges and bananas.

In my dream,
I scooped the small market of Tecuci
into a bag and carried it to Bucharest,
where I painted it on an easel
at the Children's Palace art club.

In 1989, the unfinished painting
was covered over with white paint.
Three decades later, the market itself is gone.
But I have redrawn it—
and now it will stay, just like this,
forever.

Waiting Room

In a quiet provincial station,
with a small suitcase,
I bought a ticket,
but the train had already left.
My palms were open doors.
I bought another; that one had gone too.
The platform stretched like growing hair.
Other trains came and left—
red, green, blue—
fast, local, international—
but I never managed to board a single one.
My heart ticked like the clock on the wall.
Each time, the departure hour
slipped deeper into the recent past.

A sequence nearing zero, not yet sensed.

With every ticket I bought,
a part of me slowly hardened.
My arms gently lifted
and replaced the tattered benches.
My eyes softened into squares
like little windows crowded with life.
My brain spread its anatomy
over the arrivals and departures screen.
The supporting pillars were nothing
but my limewashed legs.
In the end, only my mouth,
calling brief messages on the speaker.
I became a waiting room,
a quiet dream
where people pass through
day after day.

The Map of Childhood

This camping tent
is my grandparents' house on Dacia Street.
In the Bârlad Valley lies the sofa
where I devoured *Treasure Island.*
The compass rose smiles like a fuchsia
in the pot on the pathway.
The river flows from my Grandpa's radio,
with the main news, fixed to the eaves.
The mountain is my sister in the garden,
cooking stew for the dolls.
On these golden hills, we roamed in summer
for wild berries with our cousins.
The legend is *The Little Match Girl*,
which Grandma told us until she fell asleep.
The dotted line says: "Come to lunch now
or spoons will hang round your necks."
These dots form the string of villages
between my parents' birthplaces.
The checkered pattern murmurs
like the black-and-white TV of our cartoons.
In this emerald wetland park
I saw tigers and giraffes for the first time.
This swimmer does not stand for a pool,
but where I touched the Siret River with my toes.
This envelope is the local office
from where we used to send postcards.
This small i is me at the window of a train,
with the map of childhood shrunk
like a sticker on my forearm.

Timeless Letter

Dear Mircea,

Do you still remember me?
A blue blouse, a red skirt,
on a summer evening in Tecuci,
strolling with our grandparents on High Street,
you one way, we the other—
With my eyes like two solar eclipses
I looked straight into your heart
and we became lifelong imaginary friends.
You searched the town for me all holiday,
but I was only in your mind,
like a flag or a talisman
suspended in time, like a shiver.
I followed you everywhere, like a shadow:
to Bucharest and Calcutta,
to Paris and Chicago.
I was Maitreyi and the French exile
and the American lecture halls.
Did you think I had vanished?
I merely transform, just as you do.
I do not ask why you left,
nor why you never returned.
Let the historians seek answers.
I still wander along High Street,
I speak through time, so you won't forget
what it means when one instant
changes everything.

Yours,
A Little Girl
(about your age)

Galați

The Place of Birth

La città dove sei venuta al mondo non è qui.
Lo conferma la tua carta d'identità.

It was a long journey on a white, cold day.
You both reached the maternity ward
from a neighbouring town.
Among all the babies, only you
screamed in the dim-lit room—
a kind of rehearsal for a better life.
Every infant's cry is a country unravelling.
Some mothers give birth to maps,
to shadows and to silence.
The place of birth—two syllables
and a hollow soul, a point in another land,
on a distant continent—
And so you are always born somewhere else,
your passport, an unfinished poem,
your life, a house built only from borders,
your husband, a novel that does not know you.
Like any true mother,
you have children you never bore,
for some women create with the soul.
How fortunate that time wrote your name
with someone else's hand,
in the secret language of forest bees!

Che dolce destino, rinascere sempre altrove!
Per esempio, nel mio cuore straniero.

The City of Rebirth

I step off the train in Galați,
feel the Danube breeze
and rise from the dead
like a Roman soldier
unbothered by taxis and buses,
digital maps and buzzing alerts.
After centuries away,
I drag my wheeled bag behind me,
through communist blocks
and bare-branched trees.
It's past ten at night
and the city holds its breath.
Stray dogs bark without echo.
Am I afraid? I'm not afraid.
My hand freezes on the handle,
like gripping a sword
made for slaying dragons.
On the waterfront, the moon
sleeps turned on its side,
darkness cradling her
like a mother an unborn child.
Everything is as it was
the night I was born.
Next day, light pours in
and the river floods through my eyes.
Panta rhei, I whisper
in the tongue of my parents,
while sipping tea
and biting into the sandwich.
I touch a persimmon
and gaze through the window.
Today, I'm born again, Danube!
So like the Mississippi!

I step out like an actress
entering the theatre
through the backstage door.
In the conference hall,
someone from New York
speaks of Feng Xiaogang—
the rare flower of a dreamy generation.
I present the mayor's image
in Romanian filmography:
corrupt, laughable, cowardly—
except one woman from too long ago.
On another day,
I cross the Danube by ferry,
alongside villagers
from nearby communes.
Among dozens of sorrowful faces,
a little girl laughs.
That's all I need, a reason to hope,
to keep fighting cardboard dragons.
On the way back,
the motorboats wink at me—
do I look like a journalist?
Maybe I am.
Yes, I film the river.
Yes, I study the colour of clouds.
Yes, I interview seagulls.
I speak to the lace-like fence.
I document rust and peeling walls.
I find splendour in roses
trembling from the cold.
And in a language only I understand,
I tell myself: this is enough
for the world to come.

The Cat of Fanny Tardini

Fanny was a tempest in silk waves—
lightning in boots, thunder in gloves.
Faisons de la magie! she cried,
stepping softly, then like a queen.
She smelled of violets and tobacco.
I curled beneath her makeup chair, listening
as she hummed the world, unmasked.
Men adored her; I stayed still.
She shared with me the crumbs of triumph:
fallen petals, slices of moonlight,
backstage shadows and glittering laughter.

They built the theatre from brick,
but Fanny lit sparks in stone-cold souls—
hearts trembling, curtains shivering,
chandeliers that watched and listened.
When they said *România*, she answered *scenă*.
They spoke of *război* and *granițe*,
she sang, danced and dragged Europe into town.

Nine lives have passed since then.
Today, people walk by the theatre,
noses buried in their phones.
She's long gone, I'm still here, waiting.
Every night, I can hear her—
her ghost purring
more beautifully
than applause.

Night Litany

O, Lord of waters and ruins,
of eternal return and new algorithms,
protect our hearts from infernal clamour,
from the prideful glare of pixels.

We've forgotten how to stand silent before a spire,
to feel the stone breathe and know the story
does not perish with us, but prepares our future,
hidden in old frescoes and scrolling feeds.

O, Lord of days and nights,
of wandering and ceaseless rediscovery,
drive away from us the despair
shaped by fake news.

We've forgotten what a fortress is, with its secret stairs and pit
for those who try to steal what can no longer be stolen.
Today we have no cannons, but we have drones, followers,
sun-loungers and mountains of refuse.

O, Lord of natural calamities,
of disasters born from our own hands,
turn our brittle faith into quiet trust
and our fear of death into a vigilant guard.

We've forgotten how to stand tall and to build
with bare hands and uplifted hearts.
We scream into our stories, yet at night we dream ourselves
walking barefoot through the altar where we buried our hope.

O, Lord of shared love,
of friends and the solitary,
help us not with fire, nor with flood,
but with a true gaze.

We've forgotten crenellated cheeks, handwritten letters,
the midnight tear, the unsent texts and the sleepless hours.
Have you forgotten? We've forgotten embraces,
the stroll along the promenade, the cold hands we once held.

O, Lord of acoustic tiles
and of leaps of consciousness,
clear our minds of forgetfulness
and show us signs through the labyrinth.

We've forgotten the good of the past, the toil of merchants
and master masons, who brought stone and passion from afar.
We've forgotten the starving artists who painted
the scream and the wound for a hashtag of history.

O, Lord of swallow nests
and of the depths both seen and unseen,
listen to our murmur at the edge of the tide
and let us drink from your stillness.

We've forgotten how the church burned several times,
was closed, turned into a museum, a granary,
yet it has always remained in the same place,
a heart still beating, still knowing: true beauty endures.

King Carol I at the Train Station

Hey, ghost, what are you doing here today,
among coffee machines and provincial kiosks?
Tall boots, uniform, epaulettes, cologne...
Are you waiting for a porter? Looking out for a carriage?
What do you make of these women with raffia bags
and red nails or the men in hoodies with earbuds in,
tracksuits and trainers, sipping cappuccinos
from cardboard cups, watching crime reports on TV?
You'd best return to your own century, King,
when maps unfurled like carpets at your feet
and generals clicked their heels at your command.
Round here, not even the pigeons salute you.
Now, if you happen to be hungry, grab a snack.
The self-service machines don't bite.
Don't be upset that no one bows before you,
saying, "Your Majesty, this way, please."
You, foreign king who never queued for anything,
who ruled through silences and stiff ceremonies,
why roam the waiting room now, dazed,
haunting the book machine filled with history texts?
Did you come to see how empires crumble?
To see if anyone still knows your name?
No point staring at the arrivals and departures:
fewer and fewer board these trains nowadays.
You're far too solemn, King, for our century
and it's too late for orders, too soon for statues.
But welcome all the same, ticketless traveller.
Grab yourself a bottle of water and…
Fancy a selfie together, Your Majesty?

Timişoara

News From Timişoara

The merry-go-round giggles hysterically
in the middle of the new Iulius Town,
while the fairy-tale roofs of the cathedral
whisper softly about some martyrs of the past.
The birds flit from ramshackle mansions
to stylish restaurants and heavy prison gates,
walk among dandelions by the Bega River,
whilst the football stadium floodlights

warmly greet late yellow taxis—

They are all having a change of heart
whenever snow leopards come into town,
Naser and Ali, Hemat, Omar and Amir,
moving around like your brother,
determined and sly like your grandson,
adventurous like your cousin,
sensitive and clever like your lover,
hungry and worried like your son.

Red Squirrels

If you felt alone and cheerless
and wished somebody be with you
when you take walks in the park
among pushchairs and scooters in June,
and I were a red squirrel
on the branch of a wild cherry tree
when you raised your eyes unawares
and thought of foreign gardens,
I'd let a cherry drop on your shoulder
to help you clear your mind
and sigh and feel at ease and wish
there were some red squirrels
in the park where you live.

The Green Shadow

It was a summer's day.
They lived on the edge of the city,
in a sleeper neighbourhood—
tall blocks of flats, each floor a step
toward forgetting, each apartment
a drawer where life folded itself away.
Their daughter entered a high school
in the city's heart that year.
They traded places, moving into a house
wrapped in a wide, breathing garden.

On the day they arrived,
a blackbird shattered the silence
with its otherworldly thrill,
to the dismay of a tricolored cat.
That first night, the translator dreamed
of a green shadow, searching
for her gaze, halting at the window.
The next morning, she stepped outside
and met the walnut tree—
a breath from beyond time itself.
From then on, each daybreak,
she would check if the tree still stood
at her window, sometimes greeting it
like an old neighbour and he would answer,
whispering softly through his leaves.
Seasons passed, and the walnut
knew how to filter the fierce summer light,
how to cast shade and coolness,
how to shield the house
from autumn winds and winter snow,
wrapping it in quiet patience.

The translator had never seen a tree die.
Until one day, when the walnut
began to darken, swallowing its own sap,
its roots and the soil around them
reeking of gasoline.
In those days, trees were guarded by law—
you could not fell them on a whim.
The laws were mighty
and the people were small.
The walnut blocked the passage of cars.
On the day they began cutting,
the translator fled the city for a whole week
cradling the silence of the tree.

Pietà

She held the silence to her chest,
her son folded into memory—
not yet twenty,
his heartbeat still echoing
like a trapped bird.

I met her on the train,
eyes unblinking—
no statue, no candle, no anthem
could carry his weight—
only her hands,
clenched around absence,
swaying him still.

Her hair streamed smoke,
her palms bled calendars,
each tear a streetlamp shattered.

She whispered:
"My son is a star
the tanks forgot to crush—
he hovers above the square,
a lantern the bullets missed."

I sat across from her,
the train drifting like a cradle
for a child who would not wake.

The Poem on the Bega

Inspired by Ecaterina Vrană's paintings and diary.

Here there is death, not mere absence.
Life pulses, primordial, stubborn.
The verses have no timetable,
but tumble like dice between what we are
and what we can become.
Some drift along the riverbank with a cross painted
in pink or cobalt, emerald or saffron.
It is called art, Lat. *ars, -tis*.

01100001 01110010 01110100

The countess with cats, the green-lipped countess,
the countess watering invisible blooms.
How did we become so unsure?
On cloudy nights or moonless ones,
snowmen turn nearly black.
So too the snow-women, sipping bitter coffee
in paintings tucked away
in private collections across the ocean.

Constanța

A Coffee with Ovid

I meet him near the pastry stand—
white robe, no shoes, very chill.
"You're Ovid, right?"
"Depends who's asking", he grins,
then orders a macchiato.
"Is exile always this sunny?"
"Only when no one's watching", he says.
"Did you really write all that for love?"
He shrugs. "And tax evasion."
We sit by the sea—too many seagulls
and no gladiators to pick up the garbage.
"Do you still write poems?"
"Only reviews. 'Lovely baklava.
A haunting, existential aftertaste.'"
"But seriously", I say, "what is love?"
He sips. "A metaphor people forget
to footnote." I scroll through texts
with no replies, stir my foam,
revise a simile. Inspiration cancels
last minute ("family thing").
Yet still—I write, "because love
is a perfectly good excuse
to embarrass yourself in rhyme."
Catch the 6:20? Maybe tomorrow.
Today, I'm busy composing an ode
to that African barista
who draws a heart in my foam
and spells my name almost right.
"What if I never finish my poem?"
He winks. "Perfect. Readers love
a mystery." Then he vanishes—
but not before stealing
my croissant.

Points of View

For us, Constanța
means summer holidays,
far from home, the journey to the sea
by train or down the motorway,
splashing in the waves, roasting in the sun,
the scent of boiled sweetcorn
and anchovies sizzling in oil,
the taverns of Tomis harbour,
a lost love, a new love,
mini-cruises and sand in our shoes,
pics at the museum, the mosque, the casino,
a chorus of foreign tongues,
Ovid staring deep into his own abyss,
the sting of seaweed, salt in our hair,
a taste of freedom and escape.

For Yeva, Constanța
means refugee status,
far from home, from Odesa,
a ten-hour coach ride,
the war stretched across social media
like an oil slick on the surface of the sea,
every notification—a tremor,
papers, files, stamps, signatures,
a lost life, a new life,
lawyers promising stability,
therapists naming the pain,
Romanian lessons with Slavic accents,
a properly paid job,
at least one night of good sleep,
the longing for freedom and escape.

The Story of a Shell

There was no cradle, no lullaby—
only waves and waiting.
Two cells, strangers to each other,
and a drop of life in a sea that asked for nothing.
At birth, no one screamed.
For weeks she floated, a liquid bird
with plankton wings and dreams of stone.
When called, she sank into the deep
and anchored herself with threads of sea-silk.
She learned to stay still. She asked no questions.
She didn't complain. She wove her mantle,
she burrowed, breathed, held fast, made cells.
The noise of a rushing world, the hunger for applause—
she had no idea what those things were.

I found her on Modern Beach.

No one cries when a shell dies.
The wave alone knows the muscle gone quiet.
An octopus came and struck her.
A strong current came and forced her open.
A starfish came and stole her heart.
She forgot what it meant to have access codes.
An echo tossed her onto the shore.
Her doorless house became a studio
for bacteria and the sighs of wandering algae.
She found comfort in the salt of memory.
She got used to flip-flops trampling her.
She wouldn't blink if you got cut.
In another life, she kept the storm from me.
Now, I am the storm that holds her in my palm.

Twilight

A swan drifts on the sea—
thousands of waves glimmer around it.
Any moment now, the drowned will surface—
mouths stuffed with cigarette ends.

We draw big hearts upon the sand
and pretend geometry is enough,
while human-tall albatrosses
tug at plastic bags with their beaks.

Genius loci runs through parallel worlds,
etched with scars yet immortal,
blind as a fried fish dropped in the sand,
posed for the profile picture.

Anchored in the sublime ecosystem,
tourists film the landscape—
and vanish with every click into the salty air,
leaving small Saharas in their wake.

Ready for new planetary cataclysms,
I play with grammar at the shore—
between those who turn away
and the child's first sight of the sea.

Beach

One summer day,
when the sun
was kind and the breeze
wore salt and song,
I found a quiet beach—
the sand was silk,
the sea was clear
and turquoise.
There,
ninety-nine horses,
roaming like shadows,
unbridled and free,
their hooves making music
on the shore.
I will not reveal
the name of the place,
not in my story,
not in your feed—
The god beneath
the waves
knows why.

II: Neil Leadbeater

Cambridge

Taking down the Stained Glass in King's College Chapel, 1939

Taking down the stained glass was like taking down
dictation. Every section was delineated
and then recorded on paper. It had
to be capable of being restored
seamless at the join.

Temporary replacements were tar-paper sheets
with occasional strips of plain glass
to let in the light. Its storyline
no longer scriptural
was of flint houses on chalk ridges—
beds of alluvial gravels—
bricks of London clay.

Looking up at the fan vaulting
we think of playing cards held in the hand,
a child's depiction of the face of the sun,
ornamental glass vases,
grey stone façades.

The acoustic of war is phenomenal—
we follow the trajectory of its echo
funnelling down the aisle—
its reality is just a window away.

Every day we do what we can
just to stay alive.

In the Fitzwilliam Museum, Cambridge

An afternoon in cool interiors.

Shunning the heat, we keep company
with the Greek and Roman statuary,
speak in whispers over Egyptian mummies,
lest we disturb the peace.
Even the art upstairs is quiet.
Italian, Flemish and Spanish Schools
adept at keeping secrets
stay within their frames.

The quiet attendants move with care
as they pace from room to room.
Sometimes they stand to ponder
as if on a point of philosophy.
Deep down they know it all—
have absorbed the wisdom of centuries.
They are the proud custodians
of all they survey.

They want to keep it that way.

The Cambridge Lodes

run eye-to-eye to infinity
low-level markers for river-runs
deep ditches in still places
blue-green algae in summer scums
whose rheens are all that remains
of nineteenth century industrial power
that once raised amazing weights
fifty tons a minute…
imagine the force in that.

At Bottisham, between Slades Farm
and a disused railway bridge
never wide enough for a fen lighter
but good for smaller craft
a chamber is all that remains.
You have to imagine the flashlock,
the timber guillotine gate,
a winding drum and a winding wheel
cogwheels with ratchets—
all the paraphernalia
that made it possible
for the passage of goods
to cut through the fens.

Here, streams slippery as eels
are hemmed in on either side
running between embankments—
communities of carr and sedge,
corridors for damselflies
pockets of gibbous duckweed
water mites for miles.

Birmingham

Leaving New Street

Beyond the tunnels there were factories and cranes,
a compendium of car parks, junk yards, tips;
bulldozers shifting history.
Tower blocks bestrode the landscape. The Monday wash,
draped over railings, dried in the midday heat.

Along the way, a series of signs in quick succession
told us where we were at: *Smethwick Rolfe Street—Smethwick*
Rolfe Street—Smethwick Rolfe Street—

The summer haze, airless and venal,
congealed with the log-jam of trade:
foundries, lighting and switchgear; dossils, plugs and valves;
they put back in place all those things
that I thought I had nearly lost:
the smell of malt from a Midlands brewery, the red marl
of the back-to-backs; a school bell in a comprehensive
ringing me back to Maths.

I lived here once, much as I lived in other towns
but none has brought me back so much as this—
nosing the scent of something gone,
the past we always miss.

Vocabularies for the Jewellery Trade

Breaking in was easy. The window locks
had rusted off and half the panes
were missing. Inside
we slogged like laggards through the lemel
and grabbed all the tools we could find:
collet blocks, bezel pushers, bick iron, drills;
our pockets bulged with binding wire
and a slew of pan-head screws.

And we ran and we ran, man to man,
the sirens ringing like steel shot
as we swung right over the wall…

—a bellyful of burrs, pin-chucks, tweezers—
the swag like blood on our hands all day
and not a jewel between us.

Birmingham Botanics

Heeling south: agapanthus in a light breeze
scrawls its signature in bright blue ink
across the boundary wall.

The glasshouses, hot as gossip,
swelter in the heat.

Office workers with sweat on their palms
flood in at noon.

Half an hour of peace
from the constant trilling of phones.

In the far corner
the foxgloves are having a field day
flaunting themselves in a riot of pink:

bells for the bees.

Selective Footage

Borodin's Prince Igor and the Polovtsian Dances
at the University of Aston in Birmingham Designate /
Art at the Ikon / Contemplating the perfect circle
in the construction of the Rotunda

Tchaikovsky 4 in the Town Hall /
the Temple of Castor and Pollux

Lunchtimes at the Barber Institute /
Barges in Gas Street Basin

Seeing Simeon Solomon's *Bacchus* /
Rossetti's *La Donna Della Finestra*
and Sandys *Morgan-Le-Fay*

Getting lost in New Street / Missing the train to
Wolverhampton then catching the next one home

Heeling hard down Oozells Street
because I liked the sound of it

Bournville and Cadbury /
What I would give for chocolate now

Wolverhampton

Unpacking Thompson's Foundry

was like peeling the wrappers
off engineering
prising crates
with burglars' jemmies
to get a lever on
cowlings for aircraft,
sponsons for tanks,
parts for Spitfires
and Blenheim Bombers,
before the business closed.

Years back your sound
was that of the weight of
a wrought-iron girder
hitting the ground
from a height.

I was a child with no idea of
what went on in the name
of drop forging.

Now, hearing of your closure,
I want to feel that thrum
hit me one last time.

Vision Express

Everything on the chart will be blurred at first.
Bear with me. Imagine you're waiting
for a No. 11 in dense fog.
The fact that it fails to show up
will bring things quickly into focus.
Take a walk down the Dudley Road.
What can you see?
Can you read the first line of shops that you come to?
Does the woman in the butcher's look faint?
Is the butcher's knife
sharper now… or now?
What does that advert say?
IF YOU CAN'T CUT IT HERE
and the line below?
YOU CAN'T CUT IT ANYWHERE
Is the future of Beatties
clearer now… or now?
Concentrate your left eye on the square.
Observe the man on horseback.
Watch the red light. Tell me when it changes to green.
Rest your chin on this. Look at the screen.
Press the handheld counter
every time you see something:

Bushbury

Tettenhall *Queen Square*

Pattingham

Lower Penn

Now for the pneumotonometer

It’ll be just like coming out of *The Moon Under Water*
into a blast of night air.
No pressure.

Renton Road Allotments

Renton Road Allotments were on the other side of town
somewhere you'd never been to
but it conjured up the conviviality
of mixing with people from different cultures
who shared a passion for plants—
the Indian amid the still expanse of Exbury hybrid azaleas;
Jamaicans with their summer squashes
huggermugger with massed astilbes
ranged between the beans
and a small child
bad-mouthing belladonna
because his father had told him
it was the only fruit in the town grounds
of which he could not eat.

Halfpenny Green Aerodrome

Breaking in through a gap in the fence
we were two tearaways
on a runway to adventure.
Testing our wings we cried ‘Chocks away!’
and ran like the wind
arms outstretched
hoping a gust at gale force eight
would sweep us off our feet.
‘Any moment,’ you said,
‘we could be airborne
on a journey to the stars’
but gravity grounded us
in the disused space.
Cool, calm and collected,
we were unflappable
trying and trying and trying again
until sense left us standing
on our own two feet.

Townwell Fold

Up and down the land
there are names for places like this:
ginnels, vennels, snickleways,
threads that run
through the eye of a needle.

These folds are all that remain
of a past that was built on yarn—
the whole of it taken
out of our hands
fleeced by the winds of change.

Fantastic Fictions

Neachells

Beyond the bounds of bridle gates
these nettles
in the stung fields:
places that would never have envisaged
process plants and machine operatives,
truck factories burning their rubber
miles down the roads.

Pool Hayes

Standing water in shimmering heat.
Juggernaut gunnera
a world away from playing fields.
Impossible to hang the future
on a hook, to smooth it down
like an arm on a sleeve,
say it is washable
at a low setting
or can only be dry-cleaned.

Summer Hayes

Vocal on the wire
birds burble their outgoing calls
stop abruptly mid-chirrup
Willenhall 37891.

New Invention

Change goes against the grain.

On the A4124 a constant flow
of steady traffic
runs right through it.

Bumble Hole

Hooked on concentration
each knows his own stretch.
In it for the long haul,
their spools, slow-paced,
reel in the afternoon.
What they are looking for
is river shimmer,
a darting shadow
to break the spell:
something to unnerve them.

This may take some time.

Perton Ridge

The day ajar with light. Driving towards
Pattingham, I pull over, stop the car,
take to the fields.
How high the wheat is this season.
Seeing the tall stems, huge husks,
nodding in the wind,
the whole patch brimful at the edges
with mallow and hawkweed
and, down among the grain stalks,
harvest mice, money spiders,
soldier beetles, a summer spinning
with yellow wagtails…

How can we not love these things?

School at Four

The 40-seater *Bella Viva* pulls into the drive.
A hoard of children clamber on board.
The race for seats is on.
A teacher brings order out of chaos—
that all-important uniform queue
before the end of the day.
A boy with a satchel
sits up front
for a wide, roadside view.

For just one evening
I want to be him again
going home.

Ormes Lane

Coming home from school
on the *Bella Viva* 40-seater
we always looked forward to
that perilous 1 in 4 gradient
on the tight hairpin bend
which our driver
took with ease.
If he couldn't turn left
at the junction
but had to wait
on the cusp of the precipice
until it was safe to proceed
we'd hear the hiss
of the air brakes
before the long way down.

We'd watch his hands
on the steering wheel
that rapid swing to the left
how did he know
how far to let it go
as it spun so lightly
like a flock of birds
flying beneath his hands?

Wolverhampton Locks

Lock 1

Chubb on my mind all day.

Years back,
this red brick building
distinct, undulled,
thrummed with the
noise of trade.

I hold my hands
a little apart to get
the long perspective:
the lock framed
by fingers and thumbs—
the span of its definition.

Lock 2

Coins slip from my hand.
One rolls so close
to the edge
that I hold my breath
at the hapless thought of it
falling into the pound.

Lock 3

What I remember is this:
A man hitting the ground running.

I wonder for a second
where he has come from

and where he is going to
and then dismiss him
on a count of ten
clean out of my mind.

Lock 4

Rain thumbing the brickwork.
Brewer's building, Victorian listed,
gutted once by fire.

The boatmen opening paddles
much as a barman
would pull a pint
watching the beer fill the glass
up to the level mark.

Lock 5

Beating the barge traffic
hands down
the dog runs on
impetuous as ever
the fastest thing
on legs.

Lock 9

I look into the Lock
but the water is stubborn
and will not yield.

No words will come today.

Lock 12

On bad weather days
this is our turning point—
something understood
between a man, a dog
and a viaduct. Obedient,
the dog bounds off
but he's not chasing
pentameters. His paws are
in much too much of a hurry
to take account of metre.

Lock 13

Briefly we mark time
until the 10.35
has worked its way
out of Wolverhampton
northbound for Crewe.

When I look into water
I look into sky.
How everything shimmers
upside down—
trees, buildings, people, birds—
a child's small balloon.

Lock 14

A barge is about to enter.
As the sluice opens
I study the water
gushing with intention.

Gnats roil in the heat.

It will be fine weather
tomorrow.

Lock 15

In the watershed of England
a night of soaking rain.

Orange hawkweed
bent double

stems fractured by storms.

Lock 17

Far from the centre,
all that nests in the soft down
is the sedge warbler
content to have found
the perfect haunt in the reedbed.
I recognize its dark brown back
and dusky legs
the distinctive stroke above each eye
milk-white on the colour chart
as I stop on the towpath

to listen to its song—
not so much an attenuated churring
but more a kind of bird-chatter
on the arable edge of town.

Lock 19

How everything thins to this:

the old husk of the city gone.

The dog dashes
after thrown sticks.

his dog day begun.

Lock 21

Bottom lock. John Brown's
toll house long since gone.

Beside the racecourse
horsepower and engine power
jockey for position.

A woodpigeon clears its throat.

A note on Lock 13: During the 1860s a series of balloon flights flying on coal gas took place at the gas works. On 5 September 1862 the world record for a balloon ascent without oxygen was set by balloonists taking off from here. The balloon, flying on coal gas, reached 37,000 feet -a record that still stands. During the two and a half hour flight, scientist James Glaisher passed out and balloonist Henry Coxwell only managed to save the day by pulling on the balloon's ripcord with his teeth after he lost the use of his hands.

Source: Clayton P. "Black Country Ramblings: Along the Old Main Line, Part 2, *The Blackcountryman* Autumn 2017. Vol. 50 No. 4 pp. 58-62.

Liverpool

Skyliner

Lunchbreaks at Circle Records
scanning through vinyl for jazz:

Chris Barber playing Panama Rag
Ottilie Patterson singing Beale St. Blues

Benny Goodman playing Sweet Georgia Brown
Sarah Vaughan singing Love me or Leave me

Quincy Jones playing Summer in the City
Ella Fitzgerald singing Jerome Kern

Oscar Peterson playing Gypsy in my Soul
Astrud Gilberto singing The Shadow of Your Smile

Stan Getz playing Desafinado
Julie London singing The Good Life

Miles Davis playing Time after Time
Peggy Lee singing Why Don't You Do Right?

Bill Evans playing Night and Day
John Coltrane playing Naima

Nat King Cole singing Let there be Love
George Shearing playing Lullaby of Birdland

Nina Simone singing My Baby Don't Care For Me
Joe Loss playing Skyliner

Unforgettable Moments

Strawberry fields / Sefton Park / Visiting the Bluecoat Chambers /
art at The Walker / the Pre-raphaelites in the Lady Lever /
the Isle of Man steam packet docked at the quayside /
Gerry and the Pacemakers singing Ferry 'cross the Mersey /
calling in at the Sudley to see Strudwick's 'St. Cecilia'
or the fanciful informality of Leighton's 'Sunny Corner' /
hearing by chance Widor's Toccata in the Anglican Cathedral /
Carl Orff's Carmina Burana at the Philharmonic Hall /
the pride of Cammell Laird /views of the Clywdian Hills
from the windows of Woolton Manor / Beatlemania at The
Cavern / Norwegian Wood

India Buildings

Eight years in the making, I give you this solid
nine storey building,
roofed in green Lombardic tiles —
whose hallowed portals I used to enter
calling in at the bank.
For three years it was my fine upstanding next door neighbour
side-by-side with Wilberforce House.

The walk through foyers with Travertine walls
never failed to impress. Its painted and coffered
saucer domes bore the weight of majesty
high above my head.

Doing business there, however small the transaction,
was like stepping into the Italian Renaissance
volta dopo volta.

The Skipping Forecast

Counting was everything whether we were steady, rising or falling.
A light wind was fine but a strong one made it harder
which is why we liked to tune in for some kind of warning.
Light, moderate or fresh was best.
Winds of 34 knots or more would send our rope into spasm.
Fog was a non-starter.
Months when the summers blazed all day
we'd long-rope skip to the well-versed chant
of *Dogger, Fisher, German Bight.*
This was our game, our landlocked song
that we sang out loud for all the skippers at sea.

Newcastle

Seeing Bede in the Port of Tyne

This stop is Bede… Please mind the gap.

Fame on the railways came late for you:
another piece of irreverence
from an ill-tutored age. Now
you are part of a branch line
travelling out from the walled city
with frequent stops in between
-a name announced like all the rest -

Felling | Hebburn | Jarrow | Bede
telling | heaven’s | hallowed | creed

to a people who remember
the greatness of the past:

the building of a fleet of vessels

shipyards that used to be
their consecrated bread.

Northern Antiquities

Housed in the Department of Archaeology
these precious artifacts:

a gilt-bronze brooch from Great Chesters
'Celtic in motif and spirit'

Middle Bronze-Age tools and weapons

a harpoon of deerhorn from Whitburn

an altar to Mithras dredged from the Tyne

facsimiles of the Franks Casket and the
Lindisfarne Gospels

sections of the Rothbury Cross

a sestertius of Hadrian

bone heddle frames, signet rings,
harness mounts...

objects still so much a now

a past that will always be with us

Favourite Things

Grey's Monument, stepping into *Windows* for
Lisa della Casa and *The Four Last Songs,*
art at the Laing, the marble-lined banking hall in
Collingwood Buildings, English bond brickwork
and evening light on attic storey windows,
Hadrian's Wall at Wallsend,
Turnbull's red-brick warehouses,
red-banded Prudham sandstone, Dog Leap Stairs,
the wall at Byker: a spine of storeys spun out of Sweden
to ride the contours of the city's ground,
sailing for Stavanger from Tyne Commission Quay,
Palmer's yards, fog on the Tyne.

Collages

Central Station. Its *port cochère* of seven arches
and all those lunette windows
lighting the rooms of offices on the upper level floor /
Newcastle cathedral. Its four flying buttresses
leaning against each other
to hold the lantern tower /
Stephenson's High Level Bridge / The swing bridge /
The parabolic Millenium Bridge with its slow
blinking eye / Navigational clearance / Staying awake
after dark to hear the sound of ships
entering the Tyne /
The station constructed on a graceful curve /
The roof above: a framework of wrought-iron ribs
formed from the curved built-up I-beams
fishplated together /
beneath the vents and skylights
the long length of an LNER
disgorging passengers
from London, Peterborough, Doncaster, York
movement at the barriers.

Song for Jenny

In the high-minded boardrooms
thumbing statistics for all we were worth:
we'd meet with planner estimators,
domestics fighting infection, caterers dishing
standard fare for a working lunch
with union reps.

No delectables there.

Dundee

The Exchange Coffee House

Once a coffee house, meeting place, library
but now, chameleon-like after so many years,
keeping up with the times.
Inside, you walk up the grand staircase,
see sections of early murals
yearn to make that grand entrance
expecting a ballroom with chandeliers
but find instead a room for reading
an eighteenth century novel —
one that is long enough
to get hopelessly lost in
on a winter's afternoon.
You stop to admire the coved ceiling
and large windows
transfixed by the view of the docks.
The city in the Sidlaw-Ochil
anticline. Climate Oceanic.

The Caird Hall

Remember those Third Programme broadcasts:
an evening concert brought to us live by the BBC
from the Caird Hall, Dundee
and how the sound of the SNO
would travel by cable to our London home
from 'somewhere up in Scotland'...
'The Land of the Brave'.

Years later, the colonnade
with two square pillars at either end
surprised me.

Greek had never come into it,
but now I had to factor it in,
conjuring the word 'i(c)onic'.

Building 01. District 10, Seabraes Yards

Amazing what can be done
with thirty-seven
recycled shipping containers.
Think Maersk, CMA—CGM,
Hapag Lloyd,
Ocean Network Express.
All those crossings,
the wait in the docks
the times they traversed the globe.
Now they are still,
anchored as offices
moored to the ground.

Inside, all at sea, we sense
the motion of waves.

Cultural Profiles

Monica Manolachi is a lecturer of English and Spanish at the University of Bucharest, Romania. As a poet, she co-authored the bilingual poetry collections *Journeys in Europe / Călătorii în Europa* (Bifrost, 2022) and *Brasília* (PIM, 2018) with Scottish poet Neil Leadbeater. She also published *Joining the dots / Uniţi punctele* (PIM, 2016), *Fragaria's stories to Magus Viridis* (Brumar, 2012) and *Roses* (Lumen, 2007). *Cultural representations of food and drinks in world literature* (2025), co-edited with Lorena Mihăeş, and *Performative identities in contemporary Caribbean British poetry* (2017) are part of her work as a researcher and critic. She has been a translator from English into Romanian for almost two decades. The retranslation of *The Secret Garden* by Frances Hodgson Burnett and *Down and Out in Paris and London* by George Orwell into Romanian are her most recent achievements. As a cultural journalist, she writes articles on literature and food in local litmags.

Neil Leadbeater is an author, poet, essayist and critic based in Edinburgh, Scotland. His work has been published widely in anthologies and journals both at home and abroad. His most recent publications are *Cityscapes and Other Poems* (Cyberwit.net, Allahabad, India, 2023) and *Cycling to the End of the World* (Cyberwit.net, Allahabad, India, 2025). He is a member of the Federation of Writers (Scotland) and one of the Burgh Poets (Stirling). He is a reviewer for several journals including *Quill & Parchment* (USA), *North of Oxford* (USA), *Ink Pantry* (UK), *The Blackcountryman* (UK), *Littoral Magazine* (UK) and *Write Out Loud* (UK). His work has been translated into Chinese, Dutch, French, Nepali, Romanian, Spanish and Swedish.

www.ingramcontent.com/pod-product-compliance
Lightning Source LLC
Chambersburg PA
CBHW022159160726
48282CB00024B/254
* 9 7 8 9 3 6 3 5 4 2 4 4 0 *